MARRIAGE GOD'S WAY WORKBOOK

A Biblical Recipe for Healthy, Joyful, Christ-Centered Relationships

Scott LaPierre

Acknowledgments

First, I want to thank Kandie Schmitz and Pam Lagomarsino for proofreading the workbook.

Second, I want to thank my good friend, associate pastor, and armor bearer, Doug Connell. He proofread the workbook and provided some content. When I asked him how he wanted to handle the contribution he made, here is part of his response:

> Here you go! I'd love for you to take it and try to develop it. You can have it. Really. I honestly don't have any interest in benefitting from it personally. I developed it with the thoroughness I did because I love you and I wanted it to benefit your intended audience. So, if you want to view it as a gift from me to you, that'd be great!

Doug, I am blessed by our friendship and the privilege of serving Woodland Christian Church with you. As the apostle Paul said, "I thank my God upon every remembrance of you" (Philippians 1:3).

Third, I want to thank my wonderful wife for all her help developing questions, proofreading—and most importantly—encouraging me. Katie, you are my best friend and the love of my life. Much of the work the Lord wants me to do for Him would never get done if not for your encouragement.

Finally, I want to thank my Lord and Savior, Jesus Christ. My prayer for *Marriage God's Way* has been that He is exalted and marriages are strengthened. I have the same desire for this workbook. May it help every husband be to his bride what Christ is to the church, and every wife be to her husband what the church should be to Christ.

TABLE OF CONTENTS

Using This Workbook

Following these guidelines will allow you to receive the most benefit:

1. The workbook contains questions for each section in *Marriage God's Way*. Read the book before looking at the corresponding questions.

2. Instead of reading a chapter of the book and then answering the questions, it is best to read one section at a time and then answer the questions.

3. Some questions are addressed to both spouses, while others are for only the husband or wife. Whatever the case, be sure to discuss all your answers with your spouse.

4. Ideally, husbands and wives should each have their own workbook and do the work together.

Expect Tension

In Chapter 2 of *Marriage God's Way*, the third section, "Embrace the Struggle" says:

> As you work through this book, recognize the tension created in your marriage is a good thing. God is introducing areas that need to be improved, and the best way to do that is by asking each other tough questions.

This will be even truer as you use this workbook. Whenever you experience tension, remember God is at work strengthening weak areas of your relationship!

Focus on the Way Your Spouse Feels

Many workbook questions contain the word "feels." This is because:

- It is not a question of whether a husband *thinks* he loves his wife. It is a question of whether his wife *feels* loved.

- It is not a question of whether a wife *thinks* she respects her husband. It is a question of whether her husband *feels* respected.

Consider these two passages from *Marriage God's Way*:

1. In Chapter 10 the sixth section, "Perception Is Reality," records: "Note the emphasis here is how a wife *feels*. A husband might insist: 'My wife is the supreme relationship in my life. She is more important than anything else.' But the wife might not feel that way. A wife's perception is her reality. It is not about what the husband says or even thinks but about what the wife feels."

2. Chapter 11 discusses wives respecting their husbands, and the fifth section, "Learning, Then Embracing" records: "A wife who does [these things] will have a husband who feels very respected."

Focus on the way your spouse feels. Then, after learning how your spouse feels, make the appropriate changes to help your spouse feel differently. The poor alternative is trying to talk your husband or wife out of feeling the way he or she feels. The section, "Embrace the Struggle," also says:

> A husband might say, "Outside of the Lord Himself, do you feel you are taking second place to anything in my life?" If a wife answers that she does not feel she is the supreme relationship in her husband's life, the husband should not try to talk her out of the way she feels or persuade her to see things differently. Likewise, a wife might ask her husband, "Do you feel I respect you?" If the husband explains how she makes him feel disrespected, the wife should not argue with her husband and try to convince him he is wrong. Instead, each spouse should listen to the other and try to make the appropriate changes.

Similarly, if your husband or wife is hurt by something you have done, do not try to make him or her feel wrong. When hearing your spouse's thoughts, commit to not interrupting or arguing. If you understand how your spouse feels, then you will learn to treat him or her the way he or she wants to be treated.

Crucify Your Flesh and Apologize the Right Way

As you continue through this workbook, you are going to hear answers that reveal:

- Your weaknesses

- Hurts you have caused

- Ways you have failed

Your flesh will flare up and threaten the work God wants to do in your marriage. Read Romans 8:13 and Galatians 5:24, and then list three ways you will need to crucify your flesh:

1.

2.

3.

Stay on guard against your sinful nature tempting you to get angry. Do not let pride have victories in your marriage! Instead, humble yourself and ask for forgiveness the right way. Some people—whether intentionally or unintentionally—act like they are apologizing, but their "apologies" are simply ways of making excuses and shifting blame. This only serves to increase frustration and hurt. Sincere apologies have the opposite effect—they diffuse aggression and prevent bitterness. Proverbs 15:1a says, "A soft answer turns away wrath" and there are not many softer answers than apologies made the right way. To do this, make sure you avoid two words:

1. Avoid the word "but." When an "apology" contains this word, it is an excuse disguised as a confession:

   • "I'm sorry, BUT if they hadn't done that…"

   • "I am sorry, BUT this happened…"

   • "I'm sorry, BUT I never would've done this if not for…"

2. Avoid the word "you." When an "apology" contains this word, it is a manipulative way for people to shift blame, and make the other person feel bad about being hurt or upset:

   • "I'm sorry YOU did this…"

   • "Well, I'm sorry YOU are mad…"

   • "I'm sorry YOU are offended…"

Instead, make sure you apologize the right way. This involves two steps:

1. First, say: "I am sorry for . . ." or "I am sorry I . . ." followed by the offense you committed.

2. Then, say: "Will you please forgive me?"

The second step is important because it:

- Shows you recognize you have done something requiring forgiveness

- Shows you are not minimizing your actions

- Engages the other person and requires a response

Finally, if your spouse asks for forgiveness and you say, "I forgive you," you are obligated to do your best to forgive the way God forgives. God does not forget our sins, but He does choose not to remember them:

- Isaiah 43:25b—I will not remember your sins.

- Jeremiah 31:34b—I will forgive their iniquity, and their sin I will remember no more.

- Hebrews 8:12 and 10:17—Their sins and lawless deeds I will remember no more.

When you say, "I forgive you," you are committing to do your best to:

- Not remember your spouse's sin

- Not hold the sin against your spouse

- Refuse to bring up the sin in the future

Although Saul was the king of Israel, a more appropriate title would be the King of Excuses. Do not be like him! Read 1 Samuel 13:1–14 and 15:1–29. What was wrong with Saul's "apologies"? What excuses did he make? Who did he blame? Provide three examples:

1.

2.

3.

Take Your Time and Pray!

There is no rush as you continue through this workbook with your spouse. Allow time for prayer and reflection. Do not rush answering questions, asking each other questions, or sharing your responses. Consider working through no more than one chapter per day. Also, plan the location and atmosphere when using this workbook:

- Would it be best to do the work over some activity, such as a meal together?

- Could it be helpful to discuss your answers while taking a walk?

- Will you be more consistent if you choose a specific time (and possibly place)?

Pray together when you begin and conclude your times together.[1] When you begin, pray specifically for:

- Graciousness and honesty in answering the questions

- Humility in receiving you spouse's criticisms

When you conclude, pray specifically for:

- Your spouse to be the husband or wife God wants him or her to be

- The Holy Spirit's help in applying what you have learned and making the appropriate changes

Finally, be sure to thank God for the gospel that equips you to have the *healthy, joyful, Christ-centered relationship* he desires for you.

---

1 If you are forced to do the workbook without your spouse, you should still pray.

Introduction

"The truth of God's Word has the power to heal
and strengthen any marriage."

What is the significance of marriage in relation to the church? In relation to society?

How can our marriages serve as evangelistic tools?

Part I

Recognize That . . .

Chapter One:
Your Marriage Reflects
Your Relationship with Christ

"When a husband knows his love, and a wife knows her submission is an act of obedience to Christ, it can be that much easier. A husband's love and a wife's submission is not a test of their obedience to their spouse. It is a test of their obedience to the Lord."

Consider your relationship with your spouse is a reflection of your relationship with Christ. What three adjectives would you use to describe your marriage?

1.

2.

3.

Are these the same adjectives you want to describe your relationship with Christ? If not, what changes do you need to make?

Two commands from the Bible give us the standard for marriage:

- Ephesians 5:25—Husbands, love your wives, just as Christ also loved the church and gave Himself for her.

- Ephesians 5:22—Wives, submit to your own husbands, as to the Lord.

Husband: Do you see your love for your wife as a reflection of your love for Christ? Why or why not?

Wife: Do you see your submission to your husband as a reflection of your submission to Christ? Why or why not?

What are common excuses people give for not obeying these commands?

Which of these excuses do you tend to use?

Trust the Holy Spirit to Help You

"If there is any area of the Christian life in which the Holy Spirit's help is necessary, it is marriage."

Marriage God's Way states that being the husbands and wives God commands us to be is intimidating and overwhelming. What other words would you use?

The first half of Ephesians 5 is about "living in the Spirit." Considering the second half of Ephesians 5 contains the marriage passage, what is the significance of the instructions in the first half?

Read John 14:16, 26, and 16:7. What three areas of your marriage most need the Holy Spirit's help?

1.

2.

3.

Read 2 Corinthians 9:8 and Philippians 2:13.

1. What "good works" do you recognize in your marriage?

2. Which works are you more naturally inclined toward, and therefore they are easier for you?

3. Which works, or areas of your marriage, do you find to be more difficult, and therefore they:

  • Require more of God's grace to abound toward you as 2 Corinthians 9:8 says?

  • Require more of God's work in you as Philippians 2:13 says?

Read Ephesians 1:18–20 and Hebrews 13:20–21.

  1. Using the language of these verses, what parts of your marriage seem dead and in need of resurrection? These could be your financial situation, intimacy, communication, or unity in parenting.

  2. When considering the power discussed in these verses, what encouragement can you take away for these "dead" areas of your relationship?

Write down the above verses on index cards or sticky notes. Post them in places where you will see them frequently, such as a mirror, dashboard, a lampstand beside your bed, the hood over your stove, or inside your iPad cover. When you see them, pray for God to show you how you can change your marriage, through changing yourself—enabled and empowered by the Holy Spirit.

We Cannot Just Sit Back

Read Romans 13:13-14. List three ways you are "making provision" for your flesh:

1.

2.

3.

Provide three practical examples of how the Holy Spirit might compel you to treat your spouse better:

1.

2.

3.

You should verbalize your appreciation for your spouse's changed behavior. Provide three examples of ways your spouse has tried to change:

1.

2.

3.

"The Holy Spirit is not going to supernaturally take control of a marriage when the individuals are not committed to putting forth the necessary effort."

"We should see ourselves working side by side with God in our marriages."

Chapter Two:
Marriage "Problems" Are Really Symptoms

"When you are not involved in the body of Christ, you will not receive the encouragement and exhortation God wants you to have."

While remembering to focus on *yourself*, if a "marriage doctor" were to examine your marriage, what are three "symptoms" he would observe?

1.

2.

3.

What does your time in God's Word look like? If you are unsatisfied with your answer, what changes should you make?

Are you involved in a church? Notice the question is not, "Do you go to church?" Or "Are you a member of a church?"

1. If you are involved in a church, in what ways do you share the marital challenges you are experiencing so God can use your church family to help you?

2. If you are not involved in a church, what changes need to be made so you can be active and involved?

Handling Frustrations

Why do marriage passages, such as Ephesians 5:22–33 and 1 Peter 3:1–7, intertwine instructions for both spouses? In other words, why should husbands and wives be familiar with Scripture's commands for their spouses?

After looking at the verses above, what things do you struggle with that are preventing you from fulfilling your role in marriage?

How can you encourage your spouse to fulfill the role God has given him or her? Provide three examples:

1.

2.

3.

What can you do to make being married to you easier? Provide three examples:

1.

2.

3.

How will you pray for your marriage differently?

Embrace the Struggle

What "recurring injuries" do you see in your marriage? In other words, what problems or conflicts do you continue to experience that need to be embraced so they can be straightened out?

Why should you expect discomfort as you and your spouse discuss the tough issues?

In what ways can this discomfort be beneficial?

God's Chastening Is Not Punishment, but a Father's Loving Discipline

In your own words, explain why some people receive "the peaceable fruit of righteousness," but others do not.

As you continue through this workbook and difficult conversations take place, what reminders do you need to tell yourself? I encourage you to go back to the beginning of the workbook and reread, "Crucify Your Flesh and Apologize the Right Way" as often as necessary.

Before beginning Part II, circle the answers that would complete the following two sentences. People familiar with your marriage would say:

1. It seems like:

    a. He is the leader in their relationship.

    b. He might be the leader in their relationship.

    c. She might be the leader in their relationship.

    d. She is the leader in their relationship.

2. It seems like she:

    a. Tries to help her husband.

    b. Might be a help to her husband.

    c. Doesn't help her husband.

Part II

Genesis 1–3:
Creation of Marriage and the Fall

Chapter Three:
God's Establishment of Adam's Headship

---

*"If we understand that man's headship began at creation,
we will see it as part of God's natural, healthy, divine plan
for husbands and wives."*

What evidence shows that God established male headship at creation?

Why is it significant that God established male headship before the fall?

What is the significance of creating Adam first and then Eve, instead of creating them as a pair as He did with the animals?

God's First Command

Why did God give the first command to Adam alone instead of both Adam and Eve?

Adam Names the Animals and Eve

What two purposes did God accomplish by having Adam name the animals?

    1.

    2.

What is the significance of God bringing Eve to Adam so he could name her?

History's First Surgery

Why did God choose to create Eve from Adam's side rather than from the "dust of the ground" as He had done with every other living creature (including Adam) up to that point?

Why does Genesis 2:24 mention a man leaving his father and mother without mentioning a woman leaving her parents too?

Why would Genesis 2:24 mention leaving father and mother when Adam and Eve had no earthly father and mother?

In a marriage ceremony, a father walks his daughter down the aisle to her groom. What biblical principle does this symbolize?

Egalitarianism Versus Complementarianism

Have you been taught a complementarian or egalitarian view of marriage? If egalitarian, are you willing to reserve judgment and openly receive what the Bible teaches about distinctions between husbands' and wives' roles and responsibilities? Why or why not?

In what ways has egalitarianism influenced Western culture?

Marriage God's Way states, "Egalitarians will insist a difference in roles and responsibilities implies a difference in equality, importance, or value." Considering what you read about complementarianism, how would you refute this statement?

Since complementarianism provides better relationships between husbands and wives, in what ways are you resisting God's design by embracing egalitarianism ideas? How are these detrimental to your marriage? What adjustments do you and your spouse need to make?

Better Together

In what ways do you and your spouse complement each other?

> *"When a husband and wife become one flesh on their wedding day, they are two people who complement and complete each other."*

List three of your spouse's strengths:

1.

2.

3.

Chapter Four:
Male Leadership Is God's Pattern

"The pattern of male leadership in the community of faith began at creation and is maintained throughout Scripture."

Considering God called men to be leaders throughout the Old Testament, what application do you see this having for the church and the home?

Queens, Priestesses, and Prophetesses

What can women learn from:

1. The evil examples set by Jezebel and Athaliah?

2. The godly examples set by Esther and Huldah?

3. The inconsistent examples set by Miriam?

Deborah the Reluctant Judge

If someone defended or promoted female leadership using Deborah as an example, how would you respond?

"Deborah affirmed the rightness of male leadership, not only looking to Barak to lead but letting him know this is what God wanted."

Wife: What lessons can you learn from Deborah?

Husband: What lessons can you learn from Barak?

The Pattern Continues Today

Think of an example for each item below, and discuss the outcome/consequences:

Husband: A time your leadership was absent.

Wife: A time your husband's leadership was absent.

Husband: A time your wife usurped your leadership.

Wife: A time you usurped your husband's leadership.

After reading chapter four, how will you view leadership roles for men and women in the church and home differently?

> *"When churches have female pastors or elders, they have rejected the teaching of God's Word."*

Chapter Five:
The Help a Man Needs

---

*"When a husband thinks about his wife, he should see her
as someone who takes him from 'not good' to 'very good.'"*

Of the five reasons why it is not good for man to be alone, which stood out to you the most? Why?

First Corinthians 11:9 says, "Man was not created for woman, but woman for man." What application does this have for your marriage?

How can a wife encourage her husband?

How has God taught you forgiveness, sacrifice, patience, and dying to self in your marriage?

How can a wife treat her husband so that he sees her as a "good thing" and as "favor from the Lord?"

A Helper Comparable to Him, God as our Ezer, The Holy Spirit as Our Helper, and The Commendable Nature of Helping

These sections contain a number of reasons a wife should be encouraged by being identified as her husband's helper. List the three that stood out to you the most:

1.

2.

3.

The world has created many false stereotypes about a wife's role in her husband's life.

Wife: How are any stereotypes tempting you to think falsely about your role as a wife? What can you do to resist these influences?

Husband: What can you do to help your wife resist being influenced by the world's stereotypes?

Help Suited to the Husband

Answer separately and then discuss your answers:

Husband: List three ways your wife helps you:

1.

2.

3.

Wife: List three ways you help your husband:

1.

2.

3.

Husband: Consider your weaknesses and list three ways you could benefit from your wife's help:

1.

2.

3.

Wife: List three ways your God-given strengths can complement your husband's needs and/or weaknesses:

1.

2.

3.

Helping Is a Two-Way Street

Answer separately and then discuss together:

Husband: If your wife is going to help you, she needs you to communicate with her. List three ways you can be a better communicator:

1.

2.

3.

Wife: List three ways you would like your husband to communicate better with you:

1.

2.

3.

Husband: List three ways you can help your wife and make her load lighter:

1.

2.

3.

Wife: List three ways you want your husband to help you and make your load lighter:

1.

2.

3.

What Does a Wife's Help Look Like Practically?

Answer separately and then discuss together:

> Wife: In what ways are you tempted to be busy with the affairs of others? How does social media play a role in this temptation? What do you need to do to resist this temptation?

"The Proverbs 31 woman is busy with her own house and her own family's affairs—not the houses or affairs of others."

> Husband: Does your wife seem busy with the affairs of others? If so, what changes should she make, and how can you help her make these changes?

> Wife: List three of your strengths and weaknesses when it comes to managing the home.

> Strengths:
>
>   1.
>
>   2.
>
>   3.
>
> Weaknesses:
>
>   1.
>
>   2.
>
>   3.

Husband: List three of your wife's strengths and weaknesses when it comes to managing the home.

Strengths:

    1.

    2.

    3.

Weaknesses:

    1.

    2.

    3.

Husband: List three specific areas of the home you would like your wife to focus on:

    1.

    2.

    3.

How will you work together to strengthen these weaknesses and focus on these areas?

"Whatever activity a wife participates in outside the home should never take priority over her home or family."

Answer separately and then discuss together:

Wife: Does anything in your life take priority over your husband, children, or home? If yes, what changes need to be made to make them a priority?

Husband: Does anything in your wife's life take priority over you, your children, or your home? If yes, what changes need to be made?

Praise for Such a Helper

Answer separately and then discuss together:

Husband: Do you praise your wife (to her or others)? If the answer is yes, list three examples. If the answer is no, list three praises you will strive to give your wife in the future.

1.

2.

3.

"There are not many satisfactions a woman can enjoy more than receiving her husband and children's praise for her diligence in caring for them."

Wife: Do you feel your husband praises you (to you or others)? If the answer is yes, provide three examples of him doing so. If the answer is no, what are three things you would like him to notice and praise you for to encourage you?

1.

2.

3.

Chapter Six:
Consequences of the Fall for Husbands and Wives

"As God-appointed heads of the relationship, husbands
will be held responsible for what takes places in our marriages
and in our homes . . . Even though Eve made the initial wrong choice,
the sobering fact is God still held Adam responsible."

Answer separately and then discuss together:

Wife: Consider the two choices Eve faced when the devil tempted her.
What would a present day example of this look like for you?

Husband: Consider the two choices Adam faced when Eve offered him the fruit.
What would a present day example of this look like for you?

Wife: Think of a time you did not trust your husband. How did you feel?
What were the consequences?

Husband: Think of a time your wife did not trust you. What were the consequences, and how did it make you feel?

After the fall, what was the significance of God addressing Adam, rather than Adam and Eve?

The Results of Adam and Eve's Disobedience

Describe Adam and Eve's relationship before the fall.

Describe Adam and Eve's relationship after the fall.

A Wife's Temptation to Control Her Husband

Consider the two choices Cain faced when God rejected his offering. What application does this have for you?

"The phrase 'Your desire shall be for your husband' is a curse and not a blessing . . . These words refer to a wife's temptation to control her husband."

How do you see the desire sin has for you affecting your marriage?

Answer separately and then discuss together:

Wife: Describe two times you tried to control your husband, and explain what you would do differently now:

1.

2.

Husband: Describe two times your wife tried to control you, and explain what you wish she would have done instead:

1.

2.

A Husband's Temptation to Dominate His Wife

Answer separately and then discuss together:

Husband: Describe two times you were domineering toward your wife, and explain what you would do differently now:

1.

2.

Wife: Describe two times your husband was domineering toward you, and explain how you wish he would have acted instead:

1.

2.

A Husband's Temptation to Submit to His Wife

Answer separately and then discuss together:

Husband: Describe two times (including the consequences) you were passive and submitted to your wife when you should have led. In other words, describe two times you obeyed your wife when you should have obeyed God:

1.

2.

Wife: Describe two times (including the consequences) your husband was passive and submitted to you when he should have led. In other words, describe two times your husband obeyed you when he should have obeyed God:

1.

2.

Husband: Do you struggle more with passivity or harshness, and what changes should you make?

Wife: Does your husband struggle more with passivity or harshness, and what changes should he make?

What can you do to help your husband not struggle with passivity or harshness?

The Consequences for Abraham and Ahab

A wife stirs up her husband to do evil when she feeds his anger toward someone, discourages him from doing right, or allows him to feel comfortable compromising. Answer separately and then discuss together:

Wife: Describe a time you "stirred up" your husband to do evil, and looking back, how do you wish you would have handled the situation?

"God is going to hold men responsible for what happens in their marriages. God appointed men to lead and they cannot turn around and say, 'My wife made me do it.'"

Husband: Describe a time your wife "stirred [you] up" to do evil, and looking back, how do you wish your wife would have handled the situation? How do you wish you would have handled the situation?

Wife: Describe a time you "stirred up" your husband to do good.

Husband: Describe a time your wife "stirred [you] up" to do good.

How did reading this chapter show you the impact a wife's influence can have over her husband?

Reversing the Effects of the Fall

What effects of the fall do you see most clearly in your marriage?

What commands from Scripture would allow you to reverse these effects in your marriage?

Part III

Understanding Love

Chapter Seven:
What Is Love?

"It is natural to focus on the romance—or eros—of marriage.
But in doing so, we forget that marriage should actually be
the union of two best friends."

Considering a husband is to have the same love for his wife that Christ has for the church and God has for the world, what application can you make for marriage?

Eros—Physical Attraction, *Storge*—Natural Affection, and *Phileo*—Strong Affection

List three things that stood out to you regarding these forms of love:

1.

2.

3.

Agape—A Superior Love

How would you respond if Jesus asked, "Do you love Me?"

When Jesus looks at your life, what kind of love does He see for Him?

A Wife's *Phileo*

Why would God command *agape* of a husband, but *phileo* of a wife?

What does it look like for a wife to demonstrate *phileo* for her husband?

Answer separately and then discuss together:

Husband: List three ways your wife demonstrates *phileo* for you:

1.

2.

3.

Wife: List three ways you demonstrate *phileo* for your husband:

1.

2.

3.

Husband, answer the following three questions and then share the answers with your wife:

1. Do you feel like the items on your wife's list demonstrate *phileo* for you? Why or why not?

2. What would you like your wife to do that would demonstrate *phileo* for you?

3. What does your wife do that makes you feel as though she does not *phileo* you?

Wife: After hearing your husband's answers to the previous three questions, what actions will you take or changes will you make to satisfy him? In other words, what do you need to do to be your husband's best friend?

Chapter Eight:
Characteristics of *Agape*

"Agape is not affected by a person's looks, actions, or possessions. It cannot be earned. It can only be given."

Agape is Unconditional

Briefly describe two times you witnessed the unconditional nature of *agape*. For example, a father forgiving a son who deeply hurt him or a girl helping a sister who mistreated her:

1.

2.

Describe a time when you experienced someone showing you unconditional love.

Agape is Sacrificial

Briefly describe two times you witnessed the sacrificial nature of *agape*. For example, a mother tirelessly taking care of her baby, or someone going to extremes to help a friend in need.

1.

2.

Describe a time when your spouse showed you sacrificial *agape*.

In your own words, how would you compare *agape* and *phileo*?

Agape Is God's Love for Man

What does it mean that God's love for us is both sacrificial and unconditional?

What should be our response to this wonderful reality?

What will you do differently to show *agape* to those around you?

Agape is Man's Love for Sin

What are two ways you are tempted to give in to the:

Lust of the flesh?

1.

2.

Lust of the eyes?

1.

2.

"The tragedy is that there is very little man will not sacrifice for sin."

Pride of life?

    1.

    2.

Which of the three sins above do you struggle with most?

What are three ways you can resist these temptations?

    1.

    2.

    3.

What are three ways you can help your spouse resist these temptations?

    1.

    2.

    3.

How would you have defined love (*agape*) before reading Part III and how would you define it now?

Before:

After:

Before beginning Part IV, circle the answers that would complete the following two sentences: People familiar with your marriage would say:

1. It seems like he:

    a.   Deeply loves his wife

    b.   Probably loves his wife

    c.   Might love his wife

    d.   Doesn't love his wife

2. It seems like she:

    a.   Deeply respects her husband

    b.   Probably respects her husband

    c.   Might respect her husband

    d.   Doesn't respect her husband

Part IV

Ephesians 5:25–33: A Husband's Call to *Agape* and a Wife's Call to Respect

Chapter Nine:
A Husband Should *Agape* His Wife

"The way Christ loves the church and gave Himself for her is the way a husband is commanded to love his wife and give himself for her."

What actions demonstrate Christ's *agape* for His bride, the church?

What does it look like for a husband to demonstrate *agape* for his wife?

Answer separately and then discuss together:

Wife: List three ways your husband demonstrates *agape* for you:

1.

2.

3.

Husband: List three ways you demonstrate *agape* for your wife:

1.

2.

3.

Wife, answer the following three questions and then share the answers with your husband:

1. Do you feel like the items on your husband's list demonstrate *agape* for you? Why or why not?

2. What would you like your husband to do that would demonstrate *agape* for you?

3. What does your husband do that makes you feel as though he does not *agape* you?

Husband: After hearing your wife's answers to the previous three questions, what actions will you take or changes will you make to satisfy her?

The True Strength Needed

"Being a husband requires having the strength to hold up the family when things are difficult and take responsibility when things do not go well."

Answer separately and then discuss together:

Husband: List three ways you need to be strong for your family:

1.

2.

3.

Wife: List three ways you want your husband to be strong for your family:

1.

2.

3.

From Monday to Saturday, list three ways your marriage looks:

Different than those of unbelievers:

1.

2.

3.

The same as those of unbelievers:

1.

2.

3.

What ways can husbands establish a Christian marriage—one that is Christ-centered?

Agape Includes Sanctifying and Cleansing

How will you both make God's Word a priority in your life together?

"A husband is at least partially responsible for the sanctification of his wife."

Answer separately and then discuss together:

Husband: List three ways you will commit to sanctifying and cleansing your wife with the Word:

1.

2.

3.

Wife: List three ways you would like your husband to sanctify and cleanse you with the Word:

1.

2.

3.

Husband: How would you like your wife to express her appreciation when you sanctify and cleanse her with the Word?

Wife: How will you express your appreciation for your husband when he sanctifies and cleanses you with the Word?

A Husband Sets the Standard for Holiness

Answer separately and then discuss together:

Husband: List three things in your home that need to be removed.

1.

2.

3.

How will you maintain a high standard of holiness?

Wife: List three things in your home that your husband needs to remove.

1.

2.

3.

How can you support your husband as he maintains a high standard of holiness?

A Husband Gets the Wife He Prepares for Himself

Answer separately and then discuss together:

Husband: What are you "reaping" from the way you have prepared your wife for yourself?

How can you transition into more of a spiritual leader to your wife?

Wife: What is your husband "reaping" from the way he has prepared you for himself?

In your responses to your husband, do you see more evidence of the "fruit of the Spirit" or the "works of the flesh" within your marriage?

A Husband's Concern for His Wife

Answer separately and then discuss together:

Husband: List two ways you show the same concern for your wife that you show for yourself, and two ways you can improve in this area.

Concern for yourself:

1.

2.

Ways to improve:

1.

2.

Wife: List two ways your husband shows the same concern for you that he shows for himself, and two ways he can improve in this area.

Concern for yourself:

1.

2.

> *"Just as Adam saw Eve as an extension of his own bone and flesh, so God wants husbands to see their wives as extensions of themselves."*

Ways to improve:

1.

2.

Nourishing and Cherishing

Answer separately and then discuss together.

Husband: List three ways you nourish and cherish your wife:

1.

2.

3.

Wife: List three ways your husband nourishes and cherishes you:

1.

2.

3.

Husband: What do you need to give up to better nourish and cherish your wife?

Wife: What can your husband do to better nourish and cherish you?

Chapter Ten:
Protecting the Sanctity of Marriage

"When a husband and wife are married,
two separate halves are glued together creating one whole."

What takes place between two individuals—mentally, emotionally, and spiritually—on their wedding day?

What takes place between married couples—mentally, emotionally, and spiritually—when they divorce?

What two responsibilities do Christians have when it comes to divorce?

    1.

    2.

If you have ever mentioned the "D" word to your spouse:

    1. Confess your sin.

    2. Ask for forgiveness.

Keep the Marriage in the Marriage

Parenting, finances, timeliness, communication, and intimacy are common areas where spouses experience unity or disunity.

List three areas of your marriage experiencing unity:

     1.

     2.

     3.

List three areas of your marriage lacking unity:

     1.

     2.

     3.

Are there friends or relatives you are tempted to run to when upset with your spouse, because you know they will side with you? If so, provide the names below, and commit to your spouse not to go to these people when experiencing marriage problems.

Seeking Godly Counsel Is the Exception

What are the two mistakes couples commonly make when they're having marriage problems?

     1.

     2.

List three godly friends you can go to for counsel when you're having marriage problems:

1.

2.

3.

The Bride's Supremacy

Answer separately and then discuss together:

Husband: Second only to Christ, is your wife the supreme relationship in your life? Why or why not?

Wife: Second only to Christ, do you feel you are the supreme relationship in your husband's life? Why or why not?

"Even though a man's father and mother have been the most important earthly relationship in his life up to his wedding day, a husband is commanded to 'leave' them to be joined to his new bride."

Perception is Reality

Answer separately and then discuss together:

Husband: Do you need to remove anything from your life so your wife does not feel like second place? If the answer is yes, explain the actions you will take to help her feel like she is your greatest priority after God.

Wife: Does anything need to be removed from your husband's life so you don't feel like second place? If the answer is yes, explain the actions you would like him to take so you can feel differently.

An Important Note for Wives

Wife: How has your husband committed to making changes to please you? Discuss what you will do to communicate your appreciation for the sacrifice(s) he's making.

The Greatest Leaving and Joining

Are there any relationships, interests, or hobbies you need to "leave" so you can better "cleave" to Christ? If the answer is yes, repent, and discuss the actions you will take.

"Having a deep and sincere love for Christ is the best way to have a deep and sincere love for our spouses."

How can you and your spouse focus on cleaving together to Christ?

Chapter Eleven:
A Wife Should Respect Her Husband

"When wives express frustrations about their husbands,
it typically sounds like: 'I don't feel that my husband loves me.
I wish my husband loved me more. He never tells me he loves me.'
When husbands express frustration, it often sounds like:
'I wish my wife respected me more. I wish my wife followed my lead.
I wish my wife supported my decisions.'"

What frustrations have you experienced in your marriage?

What frustrations do you think your spouse has experienced in your marriage?

What Respect Looks Like to a Husband

Answer separately and then discuss together:

Husband: List three ways your wife makes you feel respected:

1.

2.

3.

Wife: List three ways you make your husband feel respected:

1.

2.

3.

Husband: Are there ways your wife doesn't show you respect, but you wish she did? If yes, explain.

Wife: What changes could you make so your husband feels more respected?

What Disrespect Looks Like to a Husband

Answer separately and then discuss together:

Husband: List three ways your wife makes you feel disrespected with her attitude or actions:

1.

2.

3.

Wife: List three ways you make your husband feel disrespected with your attitude or actions:

1.

2.

3.

Wife: After learning how you make your husband feel disrespected, explain the changes you will make.

"As a wife looks for her husband's best qualities, focuses on her husband's strengths, speaks well of him to others, and praises him to their children, she will find her respect for her husband growing."

Wife: How will you focus on appreciating your husband's strengths to change your attitudes and actions?

Learning Your Husband's Respect Gauge

Answer separately and then discuss together:

Husband: List three ways your wife adapts to you:

1.

2.

3.

Wife: List three ways you adapt to your husband:

1.

2.

3.

Husband: Are there ways your wife is not adapting to you that you wish she would?
If so, explain.

Wife: After hearing your husband's answer to the previous question, what actions will you take
or changes will you make to learn his respect gauge and satisfy him?

Learning, Then Embracing

How can a wife learn to make her husband's priorities her priorities?

"Ladies, work hard to make your husband's priorities your own and to put your priorities second. And when you adapt to him, do not make him feel stupid for the way he wants things done."

Answer separately and then discuss together:

Husband: Do you have a godly vision for your family? If yes, describe that vision. If no, describe how you will develop this vision. For example: seek a mentor, pray and study God's Word, or find a sermon on the subject.

Wife: Do you feel like your husband has a godly vision for your family? If so, describe that vision.

Husband: List three areas where you recognize your wife's wisdom and ask for her counsel:

1.

2.

3.

Wife: List three areas where your husband recognizes your wisdom and asks for your counsel:

1.

2.

3.

Wife: Do you feel like your husband seeks your counsel? Why or why not? If you feel like he does not seek your counsel, specify the areas you would most like him to discuss with you.

Husband: If your wife feels like you do not seek her counsel, what changes can you make to help her feel differently?

A Portrait of Love without Respect

Answer separately and then discuss together:

Husband: Do you feel your wife pounces on you when you do something wrong like Michal did with David? Why or why not?

"In truth, it is much easier for a wife to say she loves her husband than to show it through respect."

Wife: Do you feel you pounce on your husband when he does something wrong like Michal did with David? Why or why not?

Wife: If your husband feels you pounce on him when he does something wrong, how can you handle things in the future, so he doesn't feel this way?

Husband: Describe a time you felt your wife responded appropriately when you did something wrong.

Disrespect Can Change a Husband's Feelings Toward His Wife

Answer separately and then discuss together:

Husband: In what ways have you punished your wife when she has disrespected you like David did with Michal?

Wife: In what ways do you feel your husband has punished you when you have disrespected him like David did with Michal?

Husband: Have your feelings toward your wife changed because of her disrespect? If the answer is yes, describe the disrespect. Then confess your sin of not loving your wife unconditionally and ask for her forgiveness.

Wife: Do you feel like your husband's feelings toward you have changed because of your disrespect? If the answer is yes, describe the disrespect. Then confess your sin of disrespecting your husband and ask for his forgiveness.

It Is Not an Option for Husbands or Wives

Answer separately and then discuss together:

Husband: Have you loved your wife conditionally? That is to say, have you withheld love from your wife because she did not show you the respect you desire? If the answer is yes, write a confession that seeks your wife's forgiveness and then read it to her.

"Only when two people are equally committed to obeying God's commands unconditionally will a marriage experience the health and joy God desires for it."

Wife: Have you respected your husband conditionally? That is to say, have you withheld respect from your husband, because he did not show you the love you desire? If the answer is yes, write a confession that seeks your husband's forgiveness and then read it to him.

Making Loving and Respecting Easier

Answer separately and then discuss together:

Husband: List three ways you make it harder for your wife to respect you:

1.

2.

3.

Wife: List three ways your husband makes it easier to respect him:

1.

2.

3.

List three ways he makes it harder to respect him:

1.

2.

3.

Husband: After reading your wife's lists, what will you do differently to make it easier for her to respect you?

Wife: List three ways you make it harder for your husband to love you:

1.

2.

3.

Husband: List three ways your wife makes it easier to love her:

1.

2.

3.

List three ways she makes it harder to love her:

1.

2.

3.

Wife: After reading your husband's lists, what will you do differently to make it easier for him to love you?

Part V

Understanding Submission

Chapter Twelve:
Equal Opportunity Submission

"Submission—or having a submissive spirit—is spoken of positively.
If you do not want to be a submissive person, you are going to
have a hard time following Christ."

What comes to mind when hearing the word *submission*? Are your thoughts positive or negative?

Does Scripture present submission positively or negatively?

Submission Is Not Only for Wives

Aside from marriage, in what other relationships are Christians called to submit?

Which of these is hardest for you to submit? Why?

List three times you gave up rights to be at peace with others:

1.

2.

3.

The Way We Submit Is as Important as Submitting

What are the differences between submitting outwardly and submitting inwardly?

How do your actions demonstrate your attitude about submission?

Obey the Bible, Not the World

Describe two times when you have experienced freedom by obeying God:

1.

2.

"Whenever we read the Bible, we face two choices. We can shape Scripture to fit our own desires and beliefs. Or we can allow Scripture to shape us and our thinking."

Discuss times you have:

Allowed Scripture to shape you and your thinking.

Shaped Scripture to fit your desires and beliefs.

List three examples of worldly advice you have received, and briefly discuss how it conflicted with Scripture:

1.

2.

3.

Describe a time when you obeyed God's Word even though it did not make sense to you.

The Need for Submission

Since we recognize submission is necessary for orderly leadership in so many other areas of life, why do we see such a struggle to embrace it in marriage?

Since wives are commanded to submit to their husbands five times in the New Testament, why do you think some churches and/or couples reject it?

Submission Is for When a Wife Disagrees

What are the differences between a wife respecting her husband versus submitting to him?

"Wives should be encouraged by the reality that submission does not mean supporting the idea but supporting the man behind it."

Why is submission in marriage necessary?

Answer separately and then discuss together:

Wife: Discuss the blessings of a time you submitted to your husband.

Husband: Discuss the blessings of a time your wife submitted to you.

Wife: List three actions that demonstrate your submission to your husband.

1.

2.

3.

Husband: List three of your wife's actions that demonstrate her submission to you.

1.

2.

3.

"As much as a husband should strive to hear his wife's thoughts, a wife should strive not to exasperate her husband. She should not say, 'You can't make a decision yet, because you haven't heard everything I have to say,' while presenting countless variations of the same opinion said in different ways."

Answer separately and then discuss together:

Wife: Do you feel you exasperate your husband by presenting countless variations of the same opinion stated in different ways? Why or why not?

Husband: Do you feel your wife exasperates you by presenting countless variations of the same opinion stated in different ways? If yes, discuss at least one time this took place (preferably recently).

How does the idea of equating submission to working as a team encourage you?

A Husband Can Make Submission Easier, but He Can Never Make It Easy

Answer separately and then discuss together:

Husband: List three things you do that make it easier for your wife to submit to you:

1.

2.

3.

Wife: List three things your husband does that make it easier to submit to him:

1.

2.

3.

Husband: List three things you do that make it harder for your wife to submit to you:

1.

2.

3.

Wife: List three things your husband does that make it harder to submit to him:

1.

2.

3.

Husband: What changes will you make so that it will be easier for your wife to submit to you?

Wife: How will you begin praying for your husband so that it will be easier to submit to him?

Chapter Thirteen:
What Submission Does Not Mean

---

*"Wives should see themselves under their own husbands' authority,
but not under the authority of other husbands. Even in the church,
a wife is under the authority of her husband, and her husband
is under the authority of the leadership of the church."*

Submission Does Not Mean That Wives Submit to Other Men

How does the clear Scriptural explanation of a wife's call to submit *only* to her husband change your perception of submission?

How does it provide freedom for a wife?

Submission Does Not Mean That Wives Submit to Abuse

Discuss three examples of abuse:

1.

2.

3.

Discuss three examples women might claim are abuse, but in fact are examples of them not getting their way?

1.

2.

3.

Submission Does Not Mean That Wives Submit to Sin

Provide three examples of sinful situations when a wife should not submit:

1.

2.

3.

How can a wife respect her husband's priorities when he is resistant to her participating in spiritual activities?

Submission Does Not Mean Husbands Do Not Defer to Their Wives

Answer separately and then discuss together:

Wife: Do you feel like your husband gives up his preferences for you? if so, provide three examples:

1.

2.

3.

Husband: Do you feel like you give up your preferences for your wife? If so, provide three examples:

1.

2.

3.

Submission Does Not Mean Husbands Do Not Listen to Their Wives

Answer separately and then discuss together:

Wife: Do you feel your husband values your counsel? Why or why not?

"A husband who does not listen to his wife is forfeiting one of the greatest resources God has given him."

Husband: Do you feel you value your wife's counsel? Why or why not?

Wife: Discuss a time your husband didn't value your counsel, but you feel like he should have.

Husband: Discuss a time you didn't value your wife's counsel, but now recognize you should have.

How can couples learn to work together to value the counsel and opinions of their spouse?

Submission Does Not Mean Wives Are Inferior

How does a wife's submission to her husband demonstrate the unity, equality, and oneness they should share?

What application does Jesus' relationship with His Father have for marriage relationships?

Following Jesus's Example of Submission

Contrast the submission of Jesus with the rebellion of Satan. In other words: how are Jesus and Satan opposites when it comes to authority?

How does your heart and attitude of submission reflect the heart of Christ?

Chapter Fourteen:
Putting Your Husband in a Position to Lead

"When wives recognize that it is not their God-given role to lead and place the responsibility squarely on their husbands' shoulders, they increase the likelihood their husbands will take their leadership roles seriously."

Answer separately and then discuss together:

Wife: Do you feel like you put your husband in a position to lead? Why or why not?

What actions can you take to encourage and strengthen your husband's leading?

Husband: Do you feel like your wife puts you in a position to lead? Why or why not?

Wife: Discuss a time you deliberately stepped out of the way to encourage your husband to lead. How did this make you feel, and what changes did it prompt in you?

Husband: Discuss a time your wife deliberately stepped out of the way to encourage you to lead. How did this make you feel, and what changes did it prompt in you?

Wife: In what ways do you complain about your husband not leading, but then criticize the decisions he makes or the way he does things?

Husband: In what ways does your wife complain about you not leading, but then criticizes the decisions you make or the way you do things?

Embracing Your Husband's Leadership Style

Answer separately and then discuss together:

Husband: Do you feel like your wife compares you to other men? If so, provide three examples:

1.

2.

3.

Wife: Do you feel like you compare your husband to other men? Why or why not?

Husband: Describe your leadership style or personality.

Wife: Describe your husband's leadership style or personality.

How can you embrace your husband's unique leadership strengths and personality?

It Is Not Leadership Style but a Heart for God That Matters

Considering different spiritual disciplines (prayer, Bible reading, discipling, serving, etc.), answer separately and then share your answers.

Husband: What spiritual disciplines are you regularly engaging in privately and with your family?

"Every godly man is called to pray with his family, be a student of the Word, disciple his children, and serve the body of Christ."

Wife: What spiritual disciplines do you believe your husband is engaging in privately and with his family?

Husband: In what ways do you need to grow as a spiritual leader? Which spiritual disciplines could use more work?

Wife: In what ways has your husband grown as a spiritual leader?

Which spiritual disciplines could use more work as he leads your home?

How will you pray for your husband to grow as a spiritual leader in your home?

Marriage God's Way listed some excuses husbands make to avoid fulfilling their spiritual responsibilities. Consider these excuses, answer separately, and then share your answers:

Husband: What excuses do you make?

What can you do to break free from these excuses?

Wife: What excuses does your husband make?

How will you come alongside your husband as he works to break free from those excuses?

A Wife Can Make Her Husband's Spiritual Leadership Easier—Be Encouraged To . . .

Answer separately and then discuss together:

Husband: List three specific ways you would like your wife to encourage you in your spiritual leadership:

1.

2.

3.

Wife: List three specific ways you will strive to encourage your husband in his spiritual leadership:

1.

2.

3.

Be Discouraged From . . .

Answer separately and then discuss together:

Husband: List three ways your wife discourages you in your spiritual leadership:

1.

2.

3.

Wife: List three ways you will strive not to discourage your husband in his spiritual leadership:

1.

2.

3.

"The last thing any husband needs is to hear that he does not sound like the pastor on television. The power is in God's Word and not [a] husband's teaching ability."

Part VI

**1 Peter 3:1–7:
A Wife's Beauty and a
Husband's Treatment**

Chapter Fifteen:
Winning Over Your Husband

"[A husband] may be kind, affectionate, and hold to a high moral standard; however, if he has not taken the first step of obedience—that is, the obedience of faith—then he is properly identified as disobedient."

Why does the apostle Peter equate obedience with salvation?

If a wife has a believing husband who is not as spiritually mature as she would like, how can she still find encouragement when submitting to him?

What If You Are Married to an Unbeliever?

Why should a believer stay married to an unbeliever, versus divorcing and then seeking a more spiritually compatible spouse?

Why should a believing spouse not try to force an unbelieving spouse to remain?

How can a believer still be an influence for change and repentance through faithfulness to the unsaved person?

A Wife's Nagging and a Husband's Stubbornness

Answer separately and then discuss together:

Husband: List three times you recognize you were being stubborn:

1.

2.

3.

Wife: List three times you feel like your husband was being stubborn:

1.

2.

3.

Husband: List three times you feel like your wife was nagging:

1.

2.

3.

"Husbands seem to struggle with stubbornness even more when they feel they are being nagged, and wives seem to struggle with nagging even more when they feel their husbands are being stubborn."

Wife: List three times you recognize you were nagging:

1.

2.

3.

Although a wife shouldn't nag her husband, what can a husband do or say to make it easier for his wife to resist this temptation?

How can a husband resist being stubborn when his wife's frequent reminders aggravate him?

Although a husband shouldn't be stubborn, what can a wife do or say to make it easier for her husband to resist this temptation?

How can a wife avoid nagging when she is concerned about something her husband is doing or not doing?

A Warning About Winning

Answer separately and then discuss together:

Husband: List three times you feel like your wife was manipulating you and/or wearing you down:

1.

2.

3.

Wife: List three times you recognize you were manipulating your husband and/or wearing him down:

1.

2.

3.

How does a couple lose when a wife manipulates and/or wears down her husband?

Describe the outcome from one of the times you or your spouse listed.

Winning by Godly Conduct

Answer separately and then discuss together:

Husband: To give your wife confidence in the Holy Spirit's work in your life, list three things He has convicted you of regarding being a husband:

1.

2.

3.

Wife: List three things you would like to trust the Holy Spirit to convict your husband of regarding being a husband:

1.

2.

3.

After completing the previous questions, answer these separately and then discuss together:

Husband: Your wife listed three areas in which she would like to trust the Holy Spirit to convict you. Does she model what she would like you to do by her godly conduct? Does she faithfully avoid behavior she doesn't want in your life? Explain.

Wife: You listed three areas in which you would like to trust the Holy Spirit to convict your husband. Do you model what you would like your husband to do through your godly conduct? Do you faithfully avoid behavior you don't want to see in your husband's life? Explain.

Jesus Sets the Example of Godly Conduct Versus Words

How can you demonstrate godly conduct instead of words to your spouse?

In what ways can we be like Christ when we are reviled and when we suffer?

Chapter Sixteen:
A Woman's Greater Beauty

"[A woman's] physical appearance is a good indicator of her spiritual appearance. It would not be too much to say that what comes forth on the outside was produced from the inside."

Prior to reading this introductory section, how did you view outward adornment?

How do you view it now? What has changed?

What stuck out to you the most?

Outward Appearance Is a Reflection of the Heart

Considering the four mistakes women make when it comes to outward adornment (immodesty, focusing too much, disheveled, and excessiveness), answer separately and then discuss together:

Husband: Does your wife give an appropriate or inappropriate amount of attention to her outward appearance? Why do you feel that way?

Wife: Do you give an appropriate or inappropriate amount of attention to your outward appearance? Why do you feel that way?

Husband: Do you express appreciation at the way your wife takes care of her outward appearance? Why or why not?

Wife: Do you feel your husband expresses appreciation at the way you take care of your outward appearance? If yes, do you thank him? If no, what are you doing that you wish he would notice?

Husband: Do you feel your wife makes any of the four mistakes related to outward adornment? Why or why not?

Wife: Do you feel you make any of the mistakes related to outward adornment? Why or why not?

Husband: What does your wife's outward appearance say about her heart?

Wife: What does your outward appearance say about your heart?

Greater Beauty Is Found Inwardly

Answer separately and then discuss together:

Wife: How can you focus on your inward appearance?

"Women should give attention to their outward appearance, but they should give even more attention to their inward appearance. God is more concerned with the way a woman's heart looks than with her face, hair, makeup, or clothing."

Husband: How can you help your wife focus on her inward appearance?

Husband: List three "hidden" parts of your wife's inward person you have come to appreciate about her over time.

1.

2.

3.

Wife: Which "hidden" parts of your inward person does your husband notice? Are there parts you feel like he doesn't notice, but you wish he did?

Inward Beauty Is Incorruptible

Answer separately and then discuss together:

Husband: Discuss two times your wife's inward appearance made her outwardly attractive and outwardly unattractive.

Outwardly attractive:

1.

2.

Outwardly unattractive:

1.

2.

"A woman who is loud, controlling, and obnoxious might look attractive at first, but the attractiveness will disappear quickly when the lack of inward beauty is revealed."

Wife: Discuss two times your inward appearance made you outwardly attractive and outwardly unattractive.

Outwardly attractive:

1.

2.

Outwardly unattractive:

1.

2.

How does a woman's behavior reflect her true beauty?

"Spirit" Not "Mouth"

Answer separately and then discuss together:

Husband: Describe your wife's personality (i.e. introverted, extroverted, leader, follower), and explain how it can be "gentle and quiet."

How can you help your wife in developing a gentle and quiet spirit?

Wife: Describe your personality (i.e. introverted, extroverted, leader, follower), and explain how it can be "gentle and quiet."

What do you need to do to develop a gentle and quiet spirit? How can your husband help you in this area?

God's View of Inward Beauty

What allows a woman to be beautiful in God's eyes?

What makes a woman ugly in God's eyes?

"Women should keep two truths in mind. They can be beautiful in society's eyes and ugly in God's eyes. They can be plain or even unattractive in society's eyes and very beautiful in God's eyes."

Jesus Was Not Beautiful to the World

Read Isaiah 53:2–7 and 1 Peter 2:21–24, then answer the following:

Why do you think Jesus wasn't physically attractive during His earthly life?

How did Jesus demonstrate a gentle and quiet spirit?

What can you learn from that?

Chapter Seventeen:
The Bible's "Perfect" Wife

"We could almost wonder why Sarah was chosen as an example of a godly wife at all, but the [reason is] for the most part she was a woman who respected her husband and submitted to him."

Why should Sarah being chosen as the example for wives serve as an encouragement to women?

How can Abraham and Sarah's:

Mistakes encourage you in your marriage?

Faith encourage you in your marriage?

Wives Submit Even When They Are Afraid Because They Trust God

Do you see a wife's submission to her husband as an outpouring of her trust in God? Why or why not?

"When a wife submits to her husband she is showing her trust in God."

How did Sarah respond to the "terror" of trusting her husband?

Answer separately and then discuss together:

Husband: Discuss two times you believe that submitting to you caused your wife "terror." How did she respond? Did she give in to her fear or resist it?

1.

2.

Wife: Discuss two times submitting to your husband caused you "terror." How did you respond? Did you give in to your fear or resist it?

1.

2.

Husband: What can you learn from Abraham's actions?

Wife: How does the blessing Sarah received by submitting to Abraham change things for you?

Husband: What assurances can you give your wife that you are seeking her best interest? How will you pray differently before making a decision?

Husbands Are Going to Make the Wrong Decisions, and How Husbands—and Wives—Should Respond

When husbands make a wrong decision, how should:

The husband respond?

The wife respond?

"If husbands humble themselves, accept responsibility for their actions, admit when they are wrong, and—maybe most importantly—ask for forgiveness, this will encourage wives and children to accept responsibility for their actions, admit when they are wrong, and ask for forgiveness."

The husband not respond?

The wife not respond?

Answer separately and then discuss together:

Husband: Describe two times you made the wrong decision:

How did you respond? If you regret your response, how would you respond now?

How did your wife respond? If you're displeased with her response, how do you wish she would have responded?

Wife: Describe two times your husband made the wrong decision:

How did he respond? If you're displeased with his response, how do you wish he would've responded?

How did you respond? If you regret your response, how would you respond now?

Chapter Eighteen:
A Husband Treats His Wife Well By . . .

"A husband ought to know as much as there is to know about the
woman he will be with for the rest of his life."

Answer separately and then discuss together:

Husband: Do you know more about your wife than most anything else in your life? Explain your answer.

How can you learn more about your wife so you "know" her well?

Wife: Do you feel like your husband knows more about you than most anything else in his life?

How would you like your husband to learn more about you so he "knows" you well?

Husband: List three things you believe your wife wants you to know about her:

1.

2.

3.

Wife: List three things you want your husband to know about you, and explain whether you feel he knows these things:

1.

2.

3.

Living with Her According to Knowledge

Answer separately and then discuss together:

Husband: List three ways you live with your wife according to the knowledge you have of her:

1.

2.

3.

Wife: List three ways you recognize your husband lives with you according to the knowledge he has of you:

1.

2.

3.

Husband: Considering your wife's weaknesses, list three ways she would like you to live with her in an understanding way:

1.

2.

3.

How can you encourage and guide your wife in her areas of weakness?

Wife: Considering your weaknesses, list three ways you would like your husband to live with you in an understanding way:

1.

2.

3.

Valuing Her Femininity

Answer separately and then discuss together:

Husband: List three things you value in your wife:

1.

2.

3.

Wife: List three ways your husband demonstrates that he values you:

1.

2.

3.

"Peter's message to husbands is clear: Recognize the value of your wife and honor her as a result."

Husband: Do you honor your wife? Why or why not?

Wife: Do you feel your husband honors you? Why or why not?

Wife: What could your husband do that would make you feel more honored by him?

Husband: After hearing your wife's answer to the previous question, what changes will you make?

Protecting Her

Why did God make men physically stronger than women?

Answer separately and then discuss together:

Husband: Discuss two times you abused the authority God gave you:

1.

2.

Wife: Discuss two times you feel like your husband abused the authority God gave him:

1.

2.

Husband: How do you protect your wife?

Wife: How does your husband protect you?

In what ways could your husband make you feel better protected?

Have you rejected your husband's efforts to protect you? If yes, after reading about a husband protecting his wife, has your attitude changed?

Husband: After hearing your wife's answer to the previous questions, what changes will you make?

Keeping His Prayers from Being "Chopped Down"

Answer separately and then discuss together:

Wife: Discuss three times your husband treated you in a way you believe hindered his prayers:

1.

2.

3.

"Peter specifies one particular sin that prevents God from hearing the prayers of husbands—the sin of mistreating their wives."

Husband: Discuss three times you treated your wife in a way you believe hindered your prayers:

1.

2.

3.

How has studying what Peter said about the way to treat your wife impacted you? What will you do differently?

A Husband Mistreats His Wife When He Responds in Anger

Answer separately and then discuss together:

Husband: Do you feel like your wife holds you responsible when she's suffering? Why or why not?

Wife: Do you hold your husband responsible for your suffering? Why or why not?

Husband: Do you feel like your wife is content with what God has given her, or does she covet what other women have? Explain your answer.

Wife: Are you content with what God has given you, or do you covet what other women have? Explain your answer.

Husband: List three times you responded to your wife in anger, and explain how you should have responded:

1.

2.

3.

Wife: List three times you feel your husband responded to you in anger, and explain how you wish he would have responded:

1.

2.

3.

A Husband Mistreats His Wife When He Responds in Pride

Answer separately and then discuss together:

Husband: List three times you responded to your wife in pride, and explain how you should have responded:

1.

2.

3.

Wife: List three times you feel your husband responded to you in pride, and explain how you wish he would have responded:

1.

2.

3.

Husband: Are you more tempted to respond to your wife in pride or anger? What triggers your response of either anger or pride?

Wife: Do you feel your husband is more tempted to respond to you in pride or anger? Why?

What can you do to help your husband avoid responding in pride or anger?

"Husbands, when our wives are upset, let's make sure we do not respond to them in anger because we lack patience or in pride by telling them all the wonderful things we have done for them."

Part VII

1 Corinthians 7:1–6:
A Biblical View of Intimacy

Chapter Nineteen: The Case for Intimacy

"For a true lasting relationship, the thrill and excitement of eros must be supported by a deeper, unchanging love and commitment."

Are you content with the sexual intimacy in your marriage? Why or why not?

Understanding *Eros*

What are you currently doing to cultivate *eros* in your marriage?

To cultivate greater *eros* in your marriage:

What do you need to start doing?

What do you need to stop doing?

Intimacy in Marriage Is Blessed by God

What is your basic attitude about sexual intimacy in marriage?

How has your attitude about sexual intimacy in marriage changed by reading *Marriage God's Way*?

Intimacy in Marriage Is for Enjoyment as Much as Procreation

Do you see sex as a gift from God that He wants you to enjoy with your spouse? Why or why not?

Intimacy in Marriage Is Commanded

Did you recognize intimacy in marriage is not just permitted by God, but commanded? Why or why not?

Do you withhold sexual intimacy from your spouse? Explain your answer.

Do you feel like your spouse withholds sexual intimacy from you? Explain your answer.

If you withhold intimacy from your spouse, or your spouse withholds intimacy from you, what implications does this have on your marriage?

Your Body Belongs to Your Spouse

Considering your body belongs to your spouse, list three choices you can make that will bless your spouse:

1.

2.

3.

Should You Ever Abstain?

Do you and your spouse practice any form of abstinence? If so, discuss the reason(s).

If you do—or do not—practice any abstinence:

How do you feel about the current approach you are taking?

How does your spouse feel about the current approach?

If you are not united in your view of abstinence, what changes need to be made so you can be unified?

Chapter Twenty:
When Intimacy is Threatened

"As sinful people in a fallen world, we have the potential to ruin anything good God gives us."

What threats do you see to intimacy in your marriage?

Regarding these threats:

What can you do to combat them?

What do you feel your spouse can do to combat them?

Threatened by Mismatched Desires

Do you and your spouse have different desires when it comes to sexual intimacy? If yes, describe.

If you recognize differences, how do you deal with them?

If your differences cause any tension or conflict:

What changes do you need to make?

What changes would you like to see your spouse make?

Threatened by Impurity

Regarding friendships with the opposite sex:

Do you have any you believe threaten your—or the other person's—purity? If yes, what will you do differently?

Do you feel your spouse has any threatening his/her—or the other person's—purity? If yes, discuss with your spouse.

People can take certain steps to ensure purity in their marriages. For example, they might avoid certain places, remove certain movies from their home, or install accountability software on a computer. List three things:

You can do to ensure purity in your marriage:

1.

2.

3.

You would like to see your spouse do to ensure purity in your marriage:

1.

2.

3.

Part VIII

Matthew 7:24–27:
A Strong Foundation

Chapter Twenty-One:
Building on Christ

"Just as Jesus was the Rock for Israel and is the Rock for the church, He can also be the Rock—or foundation—for our marriages."

Would you say Christ is the foundation for your marriage? Why or why not?

If you do not feel like Christ is the foundation for your marriage, what changes do you need to make as a couple?

If you do feel like Christ is the foundation for you marriage, what changes do you need to make to strengthen your marriage more?

The Storms Will Come

What can you do to be ready for those daily struggles that wear on a marriage?

List the three worst trials you have experienced as a couple and how you handled them:

1.

2.

3.

What would you do differently now?

What have you learned to prepare you for the next trial?

Chapter Twenty-Two:
The Importance of Obeying

"Jesus preached the greatest sermon in history, but those who heard and did not obey were no better off than those who never heard the teaching."

Considering the importance of obeying versus simply learning:

List three steps you are going to take to apply what you have read:

1.

2.

3.

List three steps you would like to see your spouse take to apply what s/he has read:

1.

2.

3.

List three ways you are going to help your spouse apply what s/he has read:

1.

2.

3.

Response Determines Outcome

List three outcomes you would like for your marriage:

1.

2.

3.

What responses are needed from you to see these outcomes?

What responses do you feel are needed from your spouse to see these outcomes?

Wisdom and Foolishness Is Revealed by What We Do

How would you previously have defined wisdom and foolishness?

"The questions facing your marriage: Are you going to be wise, or are you going to be foolish? Are you going to obey the instruction you have learned, or are you going to be foolish and ignore God's commands? Your wisdom or foolishness is not shown by what you know or by how many Christian marriage books you have read. Your wisdom or foolishness is shown by whether you obey what you have learned."

How would you define wisdom and foolishness now?

It is easy to be motivated by a book immediately after finishing it. List three things:

You can do to make sure you stay motivated—remain wise versus foolish—in the future:

1.

2.

3.

You would like to see your spouse do to stay motivated—remain wise versus foolish—in the future:

1.

2.

3.

How will you hold each other accountable?

Epilogue:
The Mystery of Marriage

"While Christ had disciples during His earthly ministry, He did not have a bride until He laid down His life on the cross."

In what ways is marriage a picture of Christ's relationship to the church?

The Love of Christ for His Bride

How can Christ's love for you encourage you in your marriage?

The Prayers for You

List three ways your spouse is one of the greatest blessings God has given you:

1.

2.

3.

List three ways you would like to be one of the greatest blessings God has given your spouse:

1.

2.

3.

What did you expect when you began this workbook?

How has your marriage improved since you began this workbook?

"Knowing what this life holds for us, He has given us marriage so we do not have to go through these trials alone."

About the Author

Scott LaPierre and his wife, Katie, grew up together in McArthur, California, and have been blessed with six children. After college, Scott served as an officer in the Army before becoming an elementary school teacher. While teaching, he began working part time as an associate pastor at Grace Baptist Church in Lemoore, California. When the church grew, he was hired full time and remained there until becoming the senior pastor of Woodland Christian Church in Woodland, Washington, in 2010.

Scott has a bachelor's degree in business administration and two master's degrees, one in education and the other in biblical studies. He enjoys spending time with both his home and church families and studying and teaching God's Word.

You can contact Pastor Scott, learn more about him, or subscribe to his newsletter at the following:

- E-mail: scott@scottlapierre.org

- Website: www.scottlapierre.org

- Facebook: www.facebook.com/MarriageGodsWayAuthorScottLaPierre

- Twitter: PastorWCC

Would you (or your church) like to host a Marriage God's Way Conference?

Schedule

Typically there is one session on Friday evening and four sessions on Saturday, but there is flexibility:

- All the sessions can be on Saturday for a one-day conference.

- There can be less than five sessions to allow for discussion or Q&A.

- Sessions can be split over Sunday morning, Sunday evening, and/or Wednesday evening.

Outreach

Consider viewing the conference as an outreach to strengthen the marriages of—and share Christ with—your community. Pastor Scott can set up a Facebook event page for those in the church to share with others.

Compensation

Scott is thankful to be compensated by having some number of copies of *Marriage God's Way* and the *Marriage God's Way Workbook* purchased for those attending.

If you are interested, please contact him at: scott@scottlapierre.org.

Made in the USA
Columbia, SC
17 May 2020

97334835R00085